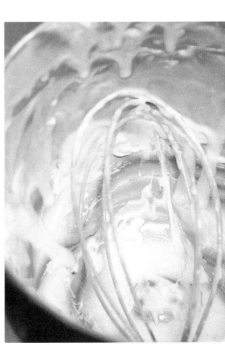

CW00959595

First published 2006 by Double Storey Books, a division of Juta & Co. Ltd, Mercury Crescent, Wetton, Cape Town

© 2006 Clare and Fiona Sprig Ras

ISBN-10: 1 77013 096 9
ISBN-13: 978 1 77013 096 9

Editing and photography by Russel Wasserfall
Design and layout by Luanne Toms
Printing by Tien Wah Press, Singapore

SPRIGS

FRESH KITCHEN INSPIRATION

BY FIONA AND CLARE RAS

Clare Ras

Fiona Ras

We've been cooking ever since we can remember, it runs in our veins. When it came to choosing a career path, there was never any doubt that we would both be chefs. Our love of food came from our mother and our desire to turn it into a successful business from our father. Sprigs opened in 1998 and all those early mornings and long hours have paid incredible dividends in attracting wonderful customers, many of whom have become firm friends who stop to chat about our favourite thing – food. It is those friends who have encouraged us to make this book. In it we share some of our favourite recipes, collected and developed throughout our careers in kitchens around South Africa and in England. The book is structured along the lines of a typical day in the Sprigs kitchen. We always start with the baking shift for bread and cakes and then move on to prep for breakfast and lunch. The end of the day is always dedicated to the catering we do for social events like book clubs and private dinners. There is a rhythm to Sprigs which has become the heartbeat of our lives. It is seasonal, like the fresh ingredients we use, and aspires to the highest standards of quality. Thanks for this are also due to our committed suppliers who tirelessly seek out the best and most unusual items for us to turn into signature dishes. There are days at Sprigs when we turn out more recipes than are included in the pages that follow. Although we love every minute we could never do it without the hard work of every one of our close-knit staff, the love of our family, and the support of our loyal customers. It is also thanks to their gentle nudging that we finally decided to produce a cookbook. This snapshot of a day in our lives, presented in the form of a recipe book, is dedicated to everyone who has made Sprigs more love than work over the years.

DAILY BREAD
THE BAKING SHIFT
STARTS THE DAY

Health Loaf

white bread flour	500g
brown bread flour	175g
sea salt	10ml
rolled oats	60g
sunflower seeds	30ml
brown sugar	15ml
active dried yeast	10g
sunflower oil	5ml
lukewarm water	1200ml
sesame seeds	15ml

Place the white flour, brown flour, salt, oats, sunflower seeds, sugar, yeast, oil and water in a large mixing bowl. Mix them together with your hands until all the flour has been incorporated, creating a sloppy, wet dough. Wrap the bowl in cling film and place it in a warm part of the kitchen until it doubles in size – this will take about 45 minutes. Pre-heat the oven to 180°C.

Grease two baking tins with a little butter and dust with flour. Divide the bread dough between the loaf tins. Sprinkle the sesame seeds onto the loaves and set aside for five minutes. Place on the middle rack of the oven and bake for 45 minutes or until an inserted skewer comes out clean. Remove from the tins and cool.

Perfectly baked loaves sound hollow when tapped with a finger

Raisin and Rosemary Bread

2 LOAVES

Whisk the yeast, honey and 100ml of the water together to dissolve the yeast and set aside for five minutes. Place the flour, salt, raisins and rosemary in a large bowl and make a well in the centre. Add the yeast liquid and the rest of the water and use your hand to mix, drawing in a little flour at a time to the centre of the well. Once the bread has formed a rough ball, tip it onto a lightly floured surface. Knead for ten minutes until the dough's surface is smooth. It should be moist but not sticky, so if it needs a bit more flour just add a little at a time. Place in a lightly greased bowl, cover with cling film and place in a warm part of the kitchen until it doubles in size – about 45 minutes. Gently deflate the dough and tip it onto a lightly floured surface and divide it in two. Roll each piece into a long sausage shape and place on a lightly greased baking tray. Sprinkle liberally with flour, cover with cling film and let it double in size again in a warm corner. Pre-heat the oven to 200°C. Half fill a teacup with water. Place the bread in the top half of the oven and place the teacup with water on a lower shelf. Bake for 20 minutes or until tapping produces a hollow sound. Cool on a rack.

active dried yeast	**10g**
honey	**5ml**
lukewarm water	**430ml**
white bread flour	**680g**
sea salt	**15ml**
raisins	**150g**
dried rosemary	**10ml**

Cream Cheese Rolls

self-raising flour	450g
sea salt	5ml
ground black pepper	2ml
red onions	2
chopped fresh herbs	125ml
smooth cream cheese	230g
egg	1
milk	230ml
cake flour for dusting	

Pre-heat the oven to 180°C. Place the self-raising flour, salt and pepper in a medium bowl. Peel and finely chop the onions and put half in a food processor with the herbs, cream cheese, egg and milk. Blitz until smooth then stir this mixture into the flour until well combined – use your hands. Tip the dough onto a lightly floured surface and lightly knead. Divide into eight and shape into smooth balls and roll in the remaining chopped onions so bits of onion stick to them. Place on a greased baking sheet dusted with flour. Brush the rolls with a little milk and bake in the oven for 25 minutes. The rolls should be golden in colour. Transfer to a wire rack and cool.

Wholemeal Soda Bread

2 LOAVES

whole-wheat flour	**700ml**
cake flour	**800ml**
salt	**15ml**
brown sugar	**60ml**
bicarbonate of soda	**10ml**
rolled oats	**60ml**
butter	**165g**
natural yoghurt	**500ml**
rolled oats	**15ml**

Pre-heat the oven to 180°C. Place the flours, salt, sugar, bicarb and 60ml of the oats in a large mixing bowl. Roughly chop the butter into cubes and rub it into the dry ingredients. Once the mixture resembles fine breadcrumbs, stir in the yoghurt. When the dough starts to come together, tip it onto a lightly floured work surface. Carefully knead, divide into two balls and place on well-floured baking sheets. Pat each loaf down lightly, sprinkle with the remaining oats and cut a cross on top. Bake for 45–60 minutes or until it sounds hollow. Cool on a wire rack. Serve with lashings of salted butter.

Quick Swedish Rye Bread

1 LOAF

light rye flour	1000ml
self-raising rice flour	
	200ml
baking powder	5ml
bicarbonate of soda	10ml
salt	15ml
cumin seeds	7ml
full cream	
natural yoghurt	500ml
milk	125ml
honey	60ml

Pre-heat the oven to 180°C. Sift the rye flour, rice flour, baking powder, bicarb and salt into a medium bowl, then stir in the cumin seeds. Tip the yoghurt, milk and honey into a small bowl and whisk together well. Stir the wet ingredients into the dry ingredients and mix until you have a wet, sticky dough. Scrape it into a 24cm cake tin greased with non-stick spray. Smooth the top of the loaf with a wet spatula. Place the bread in the oven for 30 minutes, then turn the heat down to 160°C for a further 20 minutes. Take out of the oven and cool the loaves on a cooling rack. This bread is best served the following day but may be sliced after two hours.

This is a very light rye bread which is completely wheat free

Olive Bread

active dried yeast	**10g**
honey	**5ml**
lukewarm water	**300ml**
white bread flour	**680g**
sea salt	**15ml**
olive oil	**100ml**
pitted black olives	**75g**
pitted sundried olives	**75g**

Pre-heat the oven to 200°C. Whisk the yeast, honey and 100ml of water together to dissolve the yeast. Set aside for five minutes. Place the flour, salt, olive oil, black olives and sundried olives into a large bowl and make a well in the centre. Add the yeast liquid and the rest of the water and use your hands to mix, drawing a little flour at a time to the centre of the well. Once the bread has formed a rough ball, tip it onto a lightly floured surface. Knead for ten minutes until the dough's surface is smooth. It should be moist but not sticky, so if it needs a bit more flour just add a little at a time. Place in a lightly greased bowl, cover with cling film and place in a warm part of the kitchen until it doubles in size – about 45 minutes. Gently deflate the dough and tip it onto a lightly floured surface and divide it in two. Shape each piece into a dome and place on a lightly greased baking tray dusted with flour. Cover with cling film and let it double in size again in a warm corner. Carefully brush the risen rounds with olive oil and sprinkle with sea salt. Half fill a teacup with water. Place the bread in the top half of the oven and put the teacup on a lower rack. Bake for 20 minutes or until tapping produces a hollow sound. Cool on a rack.

Sweet Potato Roti

medium sweet potato	**1**
water	
whole-wheat flour	**250ml**
brown sugar	**15ml**
salt	**2ml**
sunflower oil	
melted butter	

Peel the sweet potato and cut into chunks. Place these in a small saucepan and cover with water. Bring to the boil and simmer until tender then drain, keeping aside 60ml of the potato water. Blitz the potato in a blender until smooth. Add the flour, brown sugar, salt and 45ml of the potato water. Start slowly with the liquid, as you can always add more but you cannot take it out. Blitz until the dough comes together – you may need to add the remaining water. Place the dough on a lightly floured work surface. Knead briefly and cover with cling film to rest for 30 minutes. Divide the dough into eight balls. Carefully roll each ball into 17cm diameter discs. Heat a skillet pan and brush it with sunflower oil when it is hot. Cook each roti on one side for 15 seconds then turn and cook for two minutes. You may need to turn down the heat to medium. Remove the cooked flatbread and brush with a little melted butter. Continue to cook the remaining flatbread, cover loosely with a clean dishtowel, this will keep them warm and soft. Sweet potato flatbreads are great served with Moroccan mince curry (page 36) and great used as a wrap filled with cooked chicken breast, pesto, cream cheese, cucumber and fresh coriander.

Spice these flatbreads up with cumin seeds, chilli flakes or some ground cardamom

Brioche Loaf

Place the butter and the caster sugar in a mixer with the paddle attachment and beat for five minutes. Scrape into a bowl and set aside. Place the yeast and milk in the bowl of the mixer and whisk with a hand whisk until the yeast has dissolved. Return the bowl to the machine and, still using the paddle attachment, slowly add the salt, eggs and flour while beating on medium speed for ten minutes. Slowly add the butter mixture a little at a time. Beat for five minutes on medium speed. The dough should be glossy, elastic and shiny. Scrape into a large plastic container with a lid and set aside. You do not want to prove the brioche near too much heat as the butter will ooze out. Patience. Prove the brioche for two hours then gently deflate. Seal the lid again and place in the fridge for a minimum of four hours or overnight.

The following day place the dough on a lightly floured surface and divide into two balls. Grease two loaf tins with non-stick spray. Press down each brioche into a rectangle shape the length of the tin. Roll up like a Swiss roll and pinch the seam together. Place the seam side down in the tin. Repeat with the remaining brioche. Whisk the egg yolk and the milk together and gently brush the top of the loaves. Cover with cling film and prove until double in size, which will take two hours. Pre-heat the oven to 200°C and bake the brioche for 20 minutes, or until tapping produces a hollow sound. Remove from the tins and cool on a rack. This is a versatile bread which we use most often to make our popular French toast.

butter	**500g**
caster sugar	**45ml**
dried active yeast	**15g**
lukewarm milk	**100ml**
sea salt	**20ml**
eggs	**9**
cake flour	**750g**
egg yolk	**1**
milk	**15ml**

THE BIG BREAKFAST
WHY STOP AT BACON AND EGGS?

Baked Oats with Roast Fruit

SERVES 6

butter	**30ml**
salt	**2ml**
baking powder	**45ml**
rolled oats	**750ml**
raisins	**125ml**
sunflower oil	**125ml**
sugar	**170ml**
eggs	**2**
milk	**250ml**
ground cinnamon	**5ml**
brown sugar	**30ml**
strawberries	**250g**
peaches	**2**
plums	**4**
vanilla bean paste	**5ml**
caster sugar	**60ml**
orange juice	**100ml**
natural yoghurt	**600ml**

Grease an ovenproof dish using all the butter. In a medium mixing bowl stir the salt, baking powder, oats and raisins together. Whisk the oil, sugar, eggs and milk together and stir into the oats. Scrape into the prepared dish, sprinkle with the cinnamon and brown sugar, cover with cling film and store in the fridge overnight.

Pre-heat the oven to 180°C. Bake the oats for 20 minutes or until it is firm to the touch.

Meanwhile marinate the stoned and roughly chopped fruits with vanilla, caster sugar and orange juice for 20 minutes. When the oats come out of the oven set it to grill. Grill the fruits until they start to co-lour. Serve a spoonful of oats topped with yoghurt and the roast fruit.

You need a little time for this one as the oats should absorb the flavours and some of the liquid

Maple Bran and Banana Muffins

MAKES 12

Pre-heat the oven to 180°C. In a medium mixing bowl whisk the buttermilk, eggs, oil, syrup, melted butter, bran flakes, sugar, chopped apricots and sliced bananas together, and set aside for ten minutes.

Tip the cake flour, high fibre bran, baking powder, bicarbonate of soda and sunflower seeds into the wet ingredients and carefully stir until just combined. Be careful not to over mix the batter. Spoon into a greased muffin tin and bake for 20 minutes or until an inserted skewer comes away clean. Cool in the tins for five minutes before un-moulding and cooling on a wire rack.

buttermilk	**375ml**
eggs	**2**
sunflower oil	**60ml**
maple syrup	**80g**
butter	**60g**
bran flakes	**375ml**
brown sugar	**100g**
dried apricots	**40g**
bananas	**4**
cake flour	**110g**
high fibre bran	**125ml**
baking powder	**5ml**
bicarbonate of soda	**5ml**
sunflower seeds	**125ml**

Apple and Berry Crumble Tart

SERVES **8 – 10**

quantity sweet pastry	
(page 140)	**1**
apples	**5**
ground cinnamon	**10ml**
caster sugar	**30ml**
water	**15ml**
frozen berries	**250g**
TOPPING:	
butter	**500g**
golden syrup	**90ml**
brown sugar	**150g**
rolled oats	**150g**
desiccated coconut	**75g**
ground cinnamon	**15ml**

Pre-heat the oven to 180°C. Roll out the pastry on a lightly floured surface to line a 30cm tart tin, or two 30cm rectangular tins, and prick the base of the tart with a fork. Place in the fridge for ten minutes. Bake blind for 15 minutes or until cooked. Peel, core and roughly chop the apples and place with the cinnamon, sugar and water in a saucepan, bring to a gentle boil. Simmer until just tender. Stir in the berries and cool.

Meanwhile make the topping. Tip the butter, syrup and the brown sugar into a saucepan and heat gently. Once melted, remove from the heat and stir in the oats, coconut and cinnamon. Spoon the apple mixture into the cooked tart base. Sprinkle the topping over the tart to make a thick crust, then bake for 10 – 15 minutes or until golden in colour. Serve a wedge of the tart with natural yoghurt, fresh strawberries and a drizzle of honey.

Feta and Peppadew Muffins

MAKES 12

cake flour	**1000ml**
baking powder	**50ml**
feta cheese	**400g**
peppadews	**24**
bunch spring onions	**1**
salt and black pepper	
eggs	**4**
water	**200ml**
milk	**200ml**
butter	**100g**

Pre-heat the oven to 180°C. Tip the flour, baking powder, crumbled feta, peppadews, chopped spring onions, and salt and pepper to taste into a large bowl and lightly stir together. Whisk together the eggs, water, milk and melted butter. Stir the egg liquid into the flour carefully until just combined. Spoon into a greased muffin tin and bake for 20 minutes or until an inserted skewer comes away clean. Remove the muffins from the tin and cool.

This recipe can be halved or doubled. Try using cheddar cheese, changing the herbs and using sundried tomatoes instead of the peppadews.

Brioche French Toast

loaf brioche (page 23)	1
eggs	4
milk	30ml
caster sugar	15ml
butter	
sunflower oil	

TOPPING:
lemon curd
icing sugar

Cut 12 thick slices from the brioche. Lightly whisk the eggs, milk and sugar. Heat a non-stick frying pan and melt a little butter and oil to fry the toast in batches. Dip each slice in the egg mixture, soak for one minute and fry until golden. Lightly dust with icing sugar and serve with lemon curd.

Fiona always eats her French toast with marmalade for the sweet and sour effect

Breakfast Pie

quantity farmhouse pastry (page 140)	1
cooked back bacon	250g
Sprigs classic pesto (page 141)	45ml
grated parmesan	100g
salt and black pepper	
eggs	6
basil leaves	60ml
egg yolk	1
milk	15ml
coarse sea salt	30ml
olive oil	15ml
button mushrooms	250g
black mushrooms	250g
sprigs thyme	4
cream	500ml

Pre-heat the oven to 180°C. Roll three quarters of the pastry to line a deep 24cm tart tin. Prick the base with a fork. Start layering the filling with the bacon, followed by spoonfuls of pesto, sprinkle with grated parmesan and season with salt and pepper. Carefully tip in the eggs and torn basil leaves.

Roll the remaining pastry out and cut a disc to form a lid. Seal the edges with a fork. Lightly beat the egg yolk and milk, then brush onto the pie and sprinkle with sea salt. Bake for 45 minutes or until golden.

Heat a frying pan and fry the mushrooms and thyme for five minutes. Season with salt and pepper then pour in the cream and cook until thick. Serve the pie in wedges with a spoonful of creamy mushrooms. You can also make individual pies as we do for the restaurant.

Moroccan Spiced Mince Roti

SERVES 6

onions	2
carrots	6
red peppers	2
sunflower oil	30ml
extra lean beef	
mince	250g
garlic cloves	2
knob ginger	1
tinned tomatoes	1 x 400g
tomato puree	30ml
Moroccan spice	15ml
salt and black pepper	
eggs	6
sweet potato roti	
(page 22)	6
harissa paste	
sour cream	
fresh coriander leaves	

Peel and finely chop the onions and carrots. Seed and slice the peppers into strips and fry in the oil for five minutes. Add the mince and cook until coloured. Add the crushed garlic, grated ginger, chopped tinned tomatoes, tomato puree, Moroccan spice, salt and pepper. Bring to the boil and simmer over medium heat for 30 minutes or until reduced. Serve in a sweet potato roti topped with a soft fried egg, some harissa to taste, chopped coriander leaves and a drizzle of sour cream. Season the fried egg with salt and pepper.

As with all recipes, the better the quality of ingredients, the better the result. Use a good quality beef mince here

Bacon and Feta Fritters

SERVES 6

bacon rashers	12
self-raising flour	375ml
baking powder	5ml
feta	375ml
mixed herbs, chopped	30ml
salt and black pepper	
milk	280ml
butter	130g
eggs	5
rocket	120g
avocados	2
olive oil	
balsamic vinegar	

Cook and roughly chop the bacon and place with the flour, baking powder, crumbled feta, chopped herbs, salt and pepper in a mixing bowl. Whisk the milk, melted butter and the eggs together in a separate bowl. Stir the eggs into the flour mixture and mix until well combined. Set aside for ten minutes.

Heat a non-stick frying pan over a medium heat. Use a heaped serving spoon of batter per fritter and fry for two minutes on each side. The cooking time will depend the size of your fritter and the heat of your pan. Cook all the batter and serve two fritters per portion with sliced avocado and rocket and drizzle over a little olive oil and balsamic vinegar.

You can make smaller fritters for a cocktail snack served with a little sour cream and avocado

Omelette

eggs	2
milk	10ml
salt and black pepper	
butter	5ml
sunflower oil	5ml
filling of your choice	

IDEAS FOR FILLINGS:

chopped tomato	
Danish feta	50g
basil leaves	6
sweet chilli sauce	15ml
coriander leaves	20ml
brie	40g
cooked lentils	30ml
feta	50g
chives, snipped	10ml
peppadews	3
fontina cheese	50g
roasted brinjals	50g
pesto (page 137)	15ml

Pre-heat the grill. Whisk the eggs, milk, salt and pepper until double in volume. (At Sprigs we use a milkshake machine – it works a treat.) Heat an omelette pan and melt the butter and oil. Pour in the whisked egg mixture. Gently move the egg around the pan with a spatula. Once the egg is three quarters cooked, place the filling on one half of the omelette and place the pan under the grill for two minutes. We like to serve our omelettes slightly runny in the centre. Fold in half to serve.

We love omelettes because you can be so creative with the fillings

Bubble and Squeak Cakes

SERVES 10–12

Peel and roughly chop the potatoes and cook in boiling salted water until tender, then drain. Blanch the cabbage leaves until tender and drain well. Dry the cabbage leaves on kitchen paper and finely chop. Mash the potatoes. Heat the olive oil and fry the sliced leek until soft. Mix the mashed potato, cabbage, fried leek, butter, vinegar, salt and pepper. Press into ring moulds 7cm in diameter. Fry in a little olive oil until golden.

To make the sauce, tip the stock and wine into a medium saucepan and bring to the boil; reduce by half, add the cream and reduce by half again. Stir in the mustard, salt and pepper. Check the seasoning. Serve two cakes per person topped with a poached egg. Spoon over the mustard sauce and garnish with rocket.

potatoes	**1000g**
cabbage leaves	**450g**
olive oil	**30ml**
leek	**1**
butter	**30g**
white wine vinegar	**15ml**
salt and black pepper	
vegetable stock	**500ml**
white wine	**150ml**
cream	**100ml**
whole-grain	
mustard	**15ml**
rocket	**50g**

THE BIG LUNCH TABLE
BIG PORTIONS FOR THE LUNCH RUSH

Chicken and Sweet Potato Pie

SERVES **8**

chicken	1 x 1600g
onion	1
carrots	2
bulb garlic	1
sprigs thyme	2
sweet potatoes	6
olive oil	45ml
salt and black pepper	
butter	100g
cake flour	100g
rocket	30g
quantity farmhouse pastry (page 136)	1
milk	30ml
pumpkin seeds	60ml

Pre-heat the oven to 180°C. Place the chicken in a large saucepan and cover with water. Roughly chop the onion, carrots and garlic and add them to the saucepan with the thyme. Bring to the boil and simmer for 45 minutes or until the chicken is cooked. Remove the chicken from the saucepan and strain the liquid. You will only need one litre of stock – the remainder can be frozen.

Chop the sweet potatoes and tip into a roasting tray. Drizzle over the olive oil. Season with salt and pepper and roast for 40 minutes or until cooked.

When the chicken is cool enough to handle, remove the meat from the bone. Melt the butter in a medium saucepan, add the flour and cook for two minutes. Pour in the warm stock. Whisk until smooth and thick. Scrape into a mixing bowl, add the sweet potato, chicken, chopped rocket, salt and pepper. Stir the pie mixture well. Check the seasoning and spoon into an ovenproof dish.

Roll out the farmhouse pastry to fit the dish, place the pastry on top of the filling, press down the edges and brush with milk. Sprinkle with seeds and bake for 40 minutes or until the pastry is golden in colour and cooked.

Stock can be frozen in ice trays so that you always have some to add to sauces when cooking

Moroccan Turlu Turlu with Feta

SERVES **8**

Pre-heat the oven to 200°C. Slice the courgettes into two centimetre discs and the brinjals into 2cm cubes. Peel the onions and cut into wedges, seed and slice the peppers, peel the carrots and slice on the angle two centimetres wide. Tip the prepared vegetables into a mixing bowl and add the crushed garlic, olive oil, ground coriander seeds, allspice, drained chickpeas, passata, salt and pepper. Give it all a good stir, then transfer everything into a roasting tray and roast for 45 minutes or until the vegetables are cooked through and golden. Lightly stir in the chopped coriander and parsley, crumbled feta and serve warm or at room temperature.

courgettes	**6**
brinjals	**2**
onions	**2**
red peppers	**2**
green peppers	**2**
carrots	**6**
garlic cloves	**4**
olive oil	**45ml**
coriander seeds	**20ml**
ground allspice	**5ml**
chickpeas	**1 x 400g tin**
tomato pureé	**300ml**
salt and black pepper	
coriander leaves	**15ml**
flat-leaf parsley	**15ml**
feta cheese	**200g**

Brioche Onion Camembert Tart

SERVES **8**

quantity brioche dough	
(see page 23)	**1**
red onions	**8**
sprigs thyme	**4**
olive oil	**45ml**
salt and black pepper	
camembert	**125g**
chives	**15g**
cream	**150ml**
eggs	**2**

Make the brioche dough, but when it comes out of the fridge, make only one loaf and save the rest for the tart. Pre-heat the oven to 200°C. Peel and quarter the onions and place in a roasting tray with the thyme, olive oil, salt and pepper and roast for 20 minutes. Cool the onions slightly. Roll the dough to fit a 30cm tart tin and place in the fridge until the onions are cool. Spread the onions over the base of the dough, crumble the camembert and sprinkle the chopped chives over. Lightly whisk the cream and eggs and pour over the onions. Bake for 30–45 minutes or until the pastry is cooked and golden. Cool in the tin for five minutes before unmolding onto a plate.

This tart is incredibly rich and people always ask for the recipe

Fried Green Tomatoes

breadcrumbs	**240ml**
basil leaves	**15ml**
coriander leaves	**15ml**
Cajun spice mix	**60ml**
salt and black pepper	
green tomatoes	**8**
sunflower oil	**100ml**
natural yoghurt	**250ml**
garlic cloves	**2**
spring onions	**4**
mint leaves	**20ml**

Tip the breadcrumbs, torn basil, chopped coriander, Cajun spice, salt and pepper into a shallow dish and stir together. Core and cut the tomatoes in half horizontally and place on the breadcrumbs. Make sure they are coated in the crumbs. Heat a frying pan with the oil and fry the tomatoes over medium heat until golden.

To make the dressing, lightly whisk the yoghurt, crushed garlic, sliced spring onions, chopped mint and further seasoning together in a small bowl.

Serve the tomatoes on a platter and dollop the yoghurt mint dressing over them.

Cheesy Phyllo Pie

SERVES 8

chunky cottage cheese	**250g**
feta	**250g**
dill	**30ml**
full-cream milk	**500ml**
eggs	**4**
salt and black pepper	
melted butter	**75ml**
sheets phyllo pastry	**12**
mature cheddar	**200g**
black onion seeds	**30ml**

Pre-heat the oven to 180°C. In a medium mixing bowl stir together the cottage cheese, crumbled feta, chopped dill, milk, eggs, salt and pepper. Grate the cheddar and set aside. Brush a 25 x 36cm oven-proof dish with a little melted butter. Brush one sheet of phyllo pastry with melted butter and top with another layer of phyllo pastry. Lay the sheet on one side of the dish and repeat the phyllo pastry layer into the other side of the dish, fitting the phyllo pastry into the corners. Pour in half the cottage cheese mixture. Butter another four sheets of phyllo pastry and lay them on top of the filling, followed by the rest of the cottage cheese mixture. Top with the grated cheddar and fold in the overlapping phyllo pastry. Butter the remaining four sheets of phyllo pastry and lay them on top of the dish, pressing down lightly to seal. Brush with a little butter and sprinkle with the black onion seeds. Bake for 45 minutes or until cooked – there should be no wobble when you gently shake the dish from side to side.

Always allow ten minutes or so for pies or tarts to cool before serving

Mediterranean Courgette Tart SERVES 8

quantity farmhouse pastry (page 136)	**half**
olive oil	**15ml**
courgettes	**500g**
garlic cloves	**2**
sprigs oregano	**4**
salt and pepper	
classic pesto (page 137)	**45ml**
kalamata olives	**100g**
eggs	**2**
milk	**100ml**
Danish feta	**100g**
sun-dried tomatoes in olive oil	**200g**
basil leaves	**60ml**

Pre-heat the oven to 180°C. Roll the pastry to fit a 30cm tart tin. Chill in the fridge for ten minutes. Bake the pastry blind for ten minutes or until it is cooked through.

Heat a frying pan with the olive oil and fry the sliced courgettes for five minutes, add the crushed garlic and chopped oregano. Season with salt and pepper and set aside to cool. Spread the pesto on the base of the tart, sprinkle the pitted olives, and spread the courgettes over the olives. Beat the egg and milk together and pour over the tart. Bake for 20 minutes or until nicely browned on top. Remove from the oven. Cool for five minutes and remove from the tin.

Crumble the feta onto the tart and scatter the drained sun-dried tomatoes and torn basil leaves on top.

Thai Chilli Sweet Potatoes

SERVES **6**

sweet potatoes	**1000g**
olive oil	**45ml**
salt and black pepper	
sweet chilli sauce	**125ml**
coriander leaves	**60ml**

Pre-heat the oven to 200°C. Slice the sweet potatoes in half lengthways and then into four. Tip them into a roasting tray, drizzle with olive oil and season with salt and pepper. Toss together and roast for 45 minutes or until the potatoes are golden and crisping. Remove from the oven and pour over the sweet chilli sauce.

Cool for ten minutes then stir in the chopped coriander before spooning onto a serving plate.

We've been serving this since we opened the shop and it's still one of our most popular dishes

Beef and Lentil Bobotie

potatoes	**4**
salt and black pepper	
sunflower oil	**30ml**
onions	**2**
extra-lean beef	
mince	**750g**
garlic cloves	**4**
knob ginger	**1**
medium curry powder	
	20ml
turmeric	**20ml**
Moroccan spice	**40ml**
whole tomatoes	
	1 x 400g tin
slices white bread	**4**
milk	**250ml**
brown lentils 2 x 400g tins	
apples	**2**
flaked almonds	**200g**
raisins	**150g**
eggs	**6**
bay leaves	**6**
chutney	
fresh chilli	

Pre-heat the oven to 180°C. Cook the potatoes in salted boiling water until soft, mash with a little salt and pepper and set aside. In a medium saucepan, fry the chopped onion in the oil until soft, then add the mince and fry on high heat until nicely coloured. Add the crushed garlic, grated ginger, curry powder, turmeric and Moroccan spice. Fry for a further two minutes then add the tomatoes and cook with the lid slightly ajar for 20 minutes or until thick and well reduced. Soak the bread slices in milk while the mince is cooking, then strain and reserve the milk.

Remove the mince from the stove and stir in the strained bread, mashed potatoes, drained lentils, grated apples, almonds, raisins and check the seasoning. Spread the mince into an ovenproof dish, stud with bay leaves, whisk the milk from the bread, eggs, salt and pepper together and pour over the mince. Bake in the oven for 20 minutes or until the egg is cooked and golden in colour. Serve with chutney and chopped fresh chilli.

Asian Lamb Meatballs with Noodles

SERVES **8**

In a large bowl mix the mince, coriander, cumin, cinnamon, allspice, flour, salt and pepper and form into meatballs the size of apricots. Heat the oil in a frying pan and fry the meatballs in batches until brown and set aside. Peel and finely chop the onion and fry in the oil until they just start to colour. Add the red curry paste, fry for one minute and add the coconut milk, almonds, fish sauce and caster sugar and bring to gentle simmer. Add the meatballs and simmer until they are cooked through and the sauce has thickened.

Bring some water to the boil in a medium saucepan and cook the noodles for five minutes. Drain and add to the sauce with the lime juice and roughly chopped coriander, check the seasoning and serve.

lamb mince	**1500g**
ground coriander	**30ml**
ground cumin	**30ml**
ground cinnamon	**5ml**
ground allspice	**5ml**
cake flour	**60ml**
salt and black pepper	
sunflower oil	**120ml**
onions	**2**
red Thai curry paste	**45ml**
coconut milk	**1 x 400g tin**
ground almonds	**150g**
fish sauce	**5ml**
caster sugar	**30ml**
egg noodles	**500g**
lime juice	**30ml**
coriander leaves	

This is our own Asian version of spaghetti and meatballs and it's popular in the deli section

LUNCH WITH THE GIRLS
THE LIGHTER SIDE OF LUNCHING

Labne Pate with Curried Nuts SERVES 12

natural yoghurt	**2000ml**
salt and black pepper	
garlic cloves	**4**
Italian parsley	**60ml**
basil leaves	**60ml**
olive oil	**125ml**
flaked almonds	**50g**
cashew nuts	**50g**
sunflower oil	**30ml**
onions	**4**
curry powder	**10ml**
turmeric	**5ml**
raisins	**50g**
olive oil	

To make the labne (yoghurt cheese), strain the yoghurt overnight. To do this, scrape the yoghurt into a bowl and season with a little salt and pepper. Place a colander in a bowl, lined with a clean dish towel and pour the yoghurt into the colander. Cover the yoghurt with the overlapping cloth and leave overnight, out of the fridge.

The following day, place the strained yoghurt in a food processor. Finely slice the garlic cloves and add half to the yoghurt with the parsley and torn basil. Process until smooth. Pour in the olive oil in a steady stream with the motor still running. Check the seasoning and set aside.

Toast the flaked almonds, chop the cashews and set aside. Heat the sunflower oil and fry the finely sliced onions and remaining garlic until soft. Add the nuts and remaining ingredients and fry for two minutes. Season with salt and pepper. Serve the paté on a dinner plate with the curried onions and a drizzle of olive oil.

Savoury Cheesecake with Rocket

SERVES **8**

Pre-heat the oven to 180°C. Roll out the pastry on a lightly floured surface to fit a 20cm spring form tin or any other baking dish. Prick the base of the pastry with a fork and let it rest it in the fridge for ten minutes. Bake the pastry blind until cooked – this will take about ten minutes. Spread chutney over the base of the cooked pastry – we like to use a plum, tamarind and date chutney but you can vary it to taste. Separate the whole eggs and whisk all six egg whites until stiff. Tip the three egg yolks, lemon zest, yoghurt, sugar, cream cheese, cheddar, feta, chopped chives, salt and pepper into a medium bowl and stir together. Fold one third of the egg whites into the cheese mixture then the next third followed by the remaining egg whites and snipped chives. Scrape the filling into the cooked pastry and bake for 35–40 minutes or until firm to the touch. Let it cool slightly before you un-mould it. Serve with the rocket.

You can use any type of chutney, pesto or herbs. You could leave the base plain and serve the savoury cheesecake with a relish as an accompaniment and a side salad.

quantity farmhouse pastry (page 136)	**half**
chutney	**250ml**
whole eggs	**3**
egg whites	**3**
zest of lemon	**1**
natural yoghurt	**225ml**
caster sugar	**30ml**
cream cheese	**150g**
cheddar	**150g**
feta	**150g**
salt and black pepper	
chives	**15ml**
rocket leaves	**140g**

We based this recipe on a Mrs Beeton standard – you never know where inspiration will come from

Beetroot and Gorgonzola Salad

SERVES **6**

beetroot	**500g**
golden sultanas	**60ml**
lemon	**1**
olive oil	**15ml**
salt and pepper	
sprigs mint leaves	**4**
gorgonzola cheese	**125g**

Grate the beetroot into a bowl and stir in the sultanas, the juice of the lemon, olive oil, salt and pepper. Check the seasoning and stir in the mint leaves. Spoon onto a serving plate and garnish with crumbled gorgonzola. (A plastic packet or surgical glove will stop your hands staining when you grate the beetroot.)

Beetroot is a wonder vegetable, especially good for digestion

Brown Rice Dolmades

SERVES **8**

vine leaves in brine	**250g**
onions	**2**
garlic cloves	**2**
tomatoes	**2**
brown rice	**240g**
chickpeas	**1 x 400g tin**
Italian parsley	**30ml**
ground cinnamon	**10ml**
sliced tomatoes	**2**
olive oil	**125ml**
eggs	**6**
lemons	**2**
olive oil	**60ml**
Italian parsley	**30ml**

Soak the vine leaves in water for 20 minutes. Finely chop the onions, garlic and tomatoes and mix in a bowl with the brown rice, drained chickpeas, salt, pepper, chopped parsley and cinnamon. Drain the vine leaves. Place one leaf, vein side up on the work surface. Place one heaped teaspoon of the filling in the centre of the leaf near the stem edge. Fold the stem end up over the filling, then fold both sides towards the middle and roll up like a small cigar. Repeat with the remaining vine leaves.

Line the bottom of a saucepan with the sliced tomatoes, pack the vine leaves quite tightly on the tomatoes. Pour in the olive oil and just cover with water. Put a plate over of the rolled leaves to prevent the rolls coming undone, cover with a lid. Cook on medium heat for 60-75 minutes or until the rice is cooked. Cool in the pot. Whilst cooking check on the water as you may need to add some. Boil the eggs for eight minutes and place in cold running water before peeling. Zest and juice the lemons and whisk in the olive oil. Stir in the remaining chopped parsley. Serve the dolmades on a platter, halve the eggs and drizzle over the dressing.

Make the dolmades a day or two ahead to allow flavour to develop

Soba Noodle Mushroom Salad SERVES 8

black mushrooms	**250g**
Portabellini	
mushrooms	**250g**
lime juice	**45ml**
sesame oil	**15ml**
soy sauce	**30ml**
garlic cloves	**4**
soba noodles	**250g**
baby cucumbers	**4**
coriander leaves	**30ml**
mint leaves	**30ml**
red chillies	**2**
sweet chilli sauce	**45ml**
soy sauce	**45ml**
sesame seeds	**60ml**

Slice the mushrooms 1cm thick and tip into a medium bowl. In a small bowl whisk the lime juice, sesame oil, soy sauce and the crushed garlic together and stir into the mushrooms. Marinate the mushrooms for 30 minutes.

Meanwhile bring a saucepan of water to the boil and cook the soba noodles according to the packet instructions. Drain and set aside. Cut the cucumbers in half lengthways and then slice thinly. Roughly chop the coriander and mint and finely slice the red chilli – remove the seeds for a milder heat taste. Tip into a bowl with the sweet chilli and soy sauces, cucumber and noodles, and toss together. Arrange the noodles on a platter, top with the mushrooms and garnish with extra coriander leaves and the toasted sesame seeds.

Minted Cream Cheese Vegetable Wrap

SERVES 4

wraps	**4**
cream cheese	**140g**
mint	**30ml**
cooked butternut	**400g**
green beans	**250g**
rocket	**30g**
salt and black pepper	

Mix the cream cheese, chopped mint leaves, salt and pepper together. Blanch the green beans in salted boiling water, then refresh in ice-cold water. Heat the wraps under the grill for two minutes until they start to puff up. Spread a quarter of the cream cheese on one half of the wrap. In the middle of the wrap place a quarter of the butternut down the length. On one side place the green beans and on the other the rocket. Season with salt and pepper and roll up tightly towards the end of the cream cheese side as that is your glue. Cut in half and serve.

We often use wraps with different fillings as snacks, cut each one into five pieces

Anchovy and Herb Pasta Salad

SERVES 8 – 10

Bring a large saucepan of salted water to the boil. Cook the orecchiete until al dente -firm to the bite. Drain the anchovies and finely chop, place in a mixing bowl with the peeled and crushed garlic, finely chopped herbs, juiced lemons and stir in the olive oil. drain the pasta and tip into the dressing stirring well. Season with salt and pepper and serve.

Orecchiete pasta	**450g**
anchovies in olive oil	**100g**
garlic cloves	**4**
Italian parsley	**50g**
chives	**50g**
basil	**50g**
lemons	**2**
olive oil	**100ml**

Japanese Sesame Butternut Salad

SERVES **8**

butternut	**1000g**
peanut oil	**45ml**
sesame oil	**15ml**
salt and black pepper	
red chilli	**1**
bunch spring onions	**1**
caster sugar	**110g**
soy sauce	**15ml**
black sesame seeds	**15ml**
water	**100ml**

Pre-heat the oven to 200°C. Peel, seed and cut the butternut into 2cm cubes. Tip into a roasting dish with 15ml of the peanut oil, the sesame oil, and a little salt and pepper. Toss together and roast in the oven for 35 minutes.

Heat a wok, add the remaining peanut oil and quickly fry the chopped, seeded chilli and the sliced spring onions until slightly coloured. Add the caster sugar, soy sauce, black sesame seeds and water and bring to the boil. Cook until syrupy and reduced by one third. Drizzle the sesame syrup onto the cooked butternut and carefully toss together and serve.

Spring Onion Welsh Rarebit

10 SLICES

butter	**100g**
Dijon mustard	**60ml**
Tabasco	**2ml**
Worcester sauce	**2ml**
beer	**210ml**
camembert	**100g**
mature cheddar	**300g**
egg yolks	**2**
eggs	**2**
salt and black pepper	
bunch spring onions	**1**
asparagus	**500g**
olive oil	**30ml**
loaf Italian bread	**1**

Tip the butter, Dijon mustard, Tabasco, Worcester and beer into a medium size saucepan. Melt over gentle heat and stir in the cheeses then remove from the heat. Whisk the egg yolks and the egg, then stir into the melted cheese mixture and add the chopped spring onion. Heat the grill pan to smoking and cook the asparagus drizzled with a little olive oil and seasoned with salt and pepper. They will only take five minutes. Pre-heat the grill of the oven. Slice the bread, spoon over the Welsh rarebit and place under the grill until it starts to colour. Serve with the asparagus or with balsamic roasted cherry tomatoes.

Green Bean, Feta and Cashew Salad

SERVES 4

green beans	**250g**
olive oil	**90ml**
onions	**2**
garlic cloves	**2**
cashew nuts	**100g**
lemon	**1**
chives	**50ml**
Italian parsley	**50ml**
feta	**150g**
salt and black pepper	

Blanch the green beans in salted, boiling water. Drain. Heat the olive oil in a large frying pan, fry the sliced onion and chopped garlic until slightly coloured. Add the cashew nuts and cook until golden. Remove the pan from the heat and add the juice of the lemon, chopped herbs, feta, salt, pepper and beans. Check the seasoning and serve with cold roast chicken and a bowl of olives.

Immersing the beans in iced water stops the cooking process and retains colour

Nectarine, Rocket and Ginger Salad

To make the dressing, zest and juice the lime into a large mixing bowl and lightly whisk in the honey, chilli powder, chopped ginger, 30ml of the syrup from the ginger, olive oil, walnut oil, salt and pepper. Stone and quarter the fruit and marinate it in the dressing for 30 minutes. When you are ready to serve, toast the walnuts and add with the rocket to the fruit. Toast slices of bread, drizzle with olive oil and rub with garlic. Top each slice with a handful of salad and serve.

lime	1
honey	10ml
chilli powder	2ml
ginger in syrup	2 knobs
olive oil	30ml
walnut oil	30ml
salt and black pepper	
nectarines	10
walnuts	60ml
rocket leaves	150g
Italian bread	1 loaf
garlic cloves	2

AFTERNOON DELIGHTS
TREATS TO ENJOY
WITH TEA OR COFFEE

Biscotti

BASIC MIX:

cake flour	600g
caster sugar	600g
baking powder	20ml
eggs	6
bakers fruit mix	500g
nuts	260g

VARIATIONS:

FRUIT AND NUT

golden sultanas	100g
raisins	250g
currants	150g
pecan nuts	160g
whole almonds	100g

WHITE CHOC CHIP AND CRANBERRY

white choc chips	250g
dried cranberries	250g
pecan nuts	260g
zested lemon	1

APRICOT, FIG AND ROSEMARY

dried apricots	250g
dried figs	250g
cashew nuts	250g
dried rosemary	15ml

Pre-heat the oven to 180°C. In a bowl large, mix together the flour, caster sugar and baking powder. Stir in half the beaten eggs and mix well, then add half of what's left and mix again. Now add the last quarter a little bit at a time until the dough takes shape but isn't too wet. Add the fruit and nuts and mix well.

Grease two baking trays and divide the dough into six sausage shapes about 3cm in diameter and place at least 6cm apart. You can prevent the dough from sticking to your hands by wetting your hands with a little water. Lightly flatten the 'sausages' and bake for 20 minutes until firm to the touch and well coloured.

Remove the trays from the oven and cool for ten minutes before cutting. Set the oven to 140°C. With a serrated knife, cut the biscotti on the angle into 5–10mm slices and lay these on the oven rack. Return to the oven and cook for 30 minutes until they are pale in colour and dried out. Remove from the oven and cool. Store in an airtight container.

You can divide the dough into two instead of six and slice into long lengths.

Lavender, Orange and Olive Oil Cake

SERVES **10**

Pre-heat the oven to 180°C. Line the base of a 26cm spring form cake tin with greaseproof paper. Grease with a little butter and dust with flour. Place the bread and lavender in a food processor and whiz until finely ground. Break the eggs into a large bowl, then add the orange zest, marmalade and olive oil. Stir well with a wooden spoon until the eggs are broken up. Add the caster sugar, ground almonds and lavender breadcrumbs, and mix well. Pour into the prepared cake tin and bake in the oven for 45–50 minutes or until an inserted skewer comes away clean.

Meanwhile, make the syrup by placing the juice of the oranges, lavender honey, water and lavender flowers in a small saucepan and gently bring to the boil. Remove the lavender stalks. Pour the syrup over the cake when it is removed from the oven. Let the cake rest in the tin for ten minutes before turning it out onto a wire rack to cool. It is best to use stale bread as it absorbs more liquid. The cake lasts extremely well – about four days – and it improves with age. You can use any citrus fruit or a mixture of lemon, lime and orange.

stale bread	**55g**
lavender flowers	**10ml**
baking powder	**15ml**
eggs	**4**
orange, zested	**1**
marmalade	**45ml**
olive oil	**200ml**
caster sugar	**200g**
ground almonds	**100g**
oranges, juiced	**2**
lavender honey	**125ml**
water	**30ml**
lavender flowers	**2**

Coconut and Pecan Squares

3 DOZEN

BASE:

self-raising flour	**340g**
caster sugar	**220g**
desiccated coconut	**180g**
melted butter	**220g**

TOPPING:

eggs	**8**
vanilla essence	**10ml**
desiccated coconut	**340g**
pecan nuts	**340g**
brown sugar	**800g**
baking powder	**10ml**

Pre-heat the oven to 180°C and grease a 45 x 30cm baking tray with butter and dust with flour. For the base, mix together the flour, sugar, coconut and butter in a mixing bowl. Press the base mix into the base of the tin. Bake for ten minutes.

For the topping, lightly whisk the eggs and vanilla and set aside. Tip the coconut, pecan nuts, sugar and baking powder into a large mixing bowl and stir in the eggs with a wooden spoon. Scrape onto the cooked base and flatten the top with a spatula. Bake in the oven for 35–45 minutes or until set. Cool in the tin for ten minutes and cut into squares.

Berry and White Chocolate Cake

SERVES **8**

eggs	**4**
butter	**165g**
caster sugar	**170g**
self-raising	
rice flour	**300g**
vanilla essence	**2ml**
white chocolate	
chips	**100g**
blueberries	**250g**

GLUTEN FREE

Pre-heat the oven to 180°C. Line the base of a 22cm spring form cake tin with greaseproof paper. Grease with a little butter and dust with rice flour. Separate the eggs and whisk the egg whites until stiff and set aside. Cream the butter and sugar together until pale then add the egg yolks one at a time until well incorporated. Stir in the rice flour, vanilla and chocolate chips. Fold in the egg whites and then the blueberries. Scrape into the prepared cake tin and bake for 45–60 minutes or until an inserted skewer comes away clean. Cool in the tin for ten minutes and then un-mould and cool on a wire rack.

Clare loves finding interesting ingredients like rice flour and experimenting with them

Chocolate Frangipane Pear Tart

quantity sweet pastry
(page 136) — 1
ground almonds — 350g
butter — 230g
caster sugar — 210g
eggs — 6
cocoa — 90ml
pears — 4

Pre-heat the oven to 180°C. Roll out the pastry on a lightly floured surface to fit a 30cm tart tin and prick the base of the tart with a fork. Place in the fridge for ten minutes. Bake blind for 15 minutes or until cooked. Place the almonds, butter, sugar, eggs and cocoa into the food processor. Pulse a few times until the ingredients come together, and then scrape the filling into the cooked tart base. Slice the pears in half lengthways and then into four. Arrange them on top of the almond filling. Bake for 45 minutes or until coloured. Cool in the tin for ten minutes before removing the tart.

This recipe truly benefits from the use of quality cocoa

Tahini, Fig and Nut Cake

SERVES **8**

pitted dates	**200g**
water	**250ml**
bicarbonate of soda	**5ml**
tahini	**250ml**
caster sugar	**200g**
sunflower oil	**60ml**
bananas, roughly	
chopped	**6**
cake flour	**335g**
baking powder	**15ml**
ground ginger	**5ml**

TOPPING:

dried figs	**8**
macadamia nuts	**100g**
pecan nuts	**100g**
marmalade	**30ml**
honey	**30ml**

EGG FREE

Pre-heat the oven to 180°C. Line the base of a 26cm spring form cake tin with greaseproof paper. Lightly grease with butter and dust with flour. Tip the dates into a small saucepan and cover with the water. Bring to the boil and cook for two minutes. Remove the dates from the heat and add the bicarbonate of soda. Pour the date mixture into a mixing bowl with the tahini, caster sugar, sunflower oil and the bananas. Sift the cake flour, baking powder and ginger onto the bananas and stir well to combine. Scrape into the prepared cake tin and bake in the centre of the oven for 45–60 minutes or until an inserted skewer comes away clean. Cool in the tin for ten minutes.

Place the cake onto a plate. Tip the sliced figs, macadamia nuts, pecan nuts, marmalade and honey into a frying pan and gently heat on the stove. Cook until the nuts turn golden, stirring all the time as the nuts and honey can brown quickly. Spoon the hot figs and nuts on top of the cake and serve.

Date and Vanilla Custard Tart SERVES 10–12

quantity sweet pastry
(page 136) 1

FILLING:
pitted dates 20
egg yolks 9
caster sugar 90g
fresh cream 750ml
vanilla bean paste or
vanilla essence 5ml

Pre-heat the oven to 180°C. Roll out the pastry on a lightly floured surface to fit a 30cm tart tin and prick the base of the tart with a fork. Place in the fridge for ten minutes. Bake blind for 15 minutes or until cooked. Scatter the dates on the cooked pastry case.

For the filling, whisk the eggs yolks with the sugar in a medium bowl until light, fluffy and pale in colour. Stir in the cream and vanilla. Carefully pour the cream mixture over the dates and bake in the oven for 25–30 minutes or until set. Cool in the tin for ten minutes before removing.

Fiona has a real soft spot for custard desserts and tarts and this is one of her favourites

Strawberry Scones

cake flour	**1000ml**
baking powder	**40ml**
butter	**80g**
natural yoghurt	**250ml**
water	**125ml**
egg	**1**
strawberries	**250g**
cream	**250ml**
icing sugar	**45ml**
vanilla bean paste or	
vanilla essence	**5ml**
marscapone	**250g**

Pre-heat the oven to 190°C. Sift the flour and the baking powder into a large mixing bowl and rub in the butter until the mixture resembles fine breadcrumbs. Whisk the yoghurt, water and egg together. Hull and slice the strawberries into three and tip into the flour. Stir the yoghurt mixture into the flour loosely with a knife to bring the dough together. Transfer to the work surface and lightly roll out with a rolling pin to about 30 x 30cm in length and 4cm thick. Cut out the scones with a round pastry cutter, lay on a greased baking sheet and bake for 12–15 minutes. Cool on a rack. Lightly whisk the cream with the icing sugar to soft peaks and stir in the vanilla and mascarpone.

Using the scone base, you can experiment with other fruits, particularly berries

Lemon, Ricotta and Almond Cake

SERVES **8**

lemons	**5**
ricotta cheese	**300g**
eggs	**6**
butter	**225g**
caster sugar	**250g**
cake flour	**65g**
ground almonds	**250g**

Pre-heat the oven to 180°C. Line the base of a 26cm spring form cake tin with greaseproof paper. Grease with a little butter and dust with flour. Zest the lemons and set aside. Juice two lemons and mix with the ricotta. Separate the eggs and whisk the egg whites until stiff. Cream the butter and the sugar in a large bowl until pale. Slowly add the egg yolks one at a time. Stir in the lemon zest and fold in the flour and ground almonds. Fold in one third of the egg whites to incorporate the whites into the batter, then fold in the remaining whites and lastly fold in the lemony ricotta. Scrape into the prepared tin and bake for 45–50 minutes or until an inserted skewer comes away clean. Cool in the tin for ten minutes and then un-mould.

Lightly Spiced Courgette Cake

SERVES 10

Pre-heat the oven to 170°C. Line the base of a 26cm spring form cake tin with greaseproof paper. Lightly grease with butter and dust with a little potato flour. Separate the eggs and whisk the whites until stiff in a large grease-free bowl with a hand held mixer. Sift the potato flour, baking powder and the spices into a bowl and set aside. Tip the egg yolks into a large bowl with the sugar and whisk with a hand held mixer until thick and pale in colour. Stir in the apricot jam. Fold the egg whites into the yolk mixture and then carefully fold in the grated courgettes, flour mixture and ground almonds. Pour into the prepared cake tin and bake for about 50 minutes or until an inserted skewer comes away clean. Cool the cake in the tin for ten minutes before turning out onto a wire rack to cool. Dust with icing sugar and serve. You can replace the courgettes with grated beetroot, carrots or parsnips. This is a great wheat-free cake recipe and the cake lasts for days after it has been made.

eggs	8
potato flour	80g
baking powder	10ml
cinnamon	10ml
ground cloves	5ml
caster sugar	340g
apricot jam	30ml
courgettes	340g
ground almonds	340g
icing sugar	

WHEAT FREE

This is a wheat–free treat for gluten–intolerant people

RAUCOUS BOOK CLUB
EASY SNACKS TO SOAK UP THE WINE

Beetroot Hummus

dried chickpeas	**250g**
beetroot	**3**
garlic cloves	**3**
tahini	**100ml**
lemon juice	**60ml**
salt and black pepper	
olive oil	**100ml**
tortilla wraps	**4**

Cover the chickpeas with water and soak overnight. The following day, drain the chickpeas and tip into a medium saucepan with the roughly chopped beetroot. Cover with water. Bring to the boil and simmer until tender – this will take about 40 minutes. Remove any scum that floats to the surface.

Pre-heat the oven to 180°C. Drain the chickpea and beetroot mixture and tip into a blender with the garlic, tahini, lemon juice, salt and pepper and blitz for two minutes. Slowly pour in the olive oil. Check the seasoning. Scrape onto a platter and set aside. Cut each tortilla into eight wedges and place on an oven rack. Bake for five minutes. Serve with the hummus.

Butternut and Thyme Tatins

20 MUFFIN SIZE TATINS

Pre-heat the oven to 190°C. Grease the muffin tin with non-stick spray. Peel and finely slice the butternut and place in a bowl. Add the thyme leaves, season with salt and pepper and toss together. Roll out the puff pastry on a lightly floured surface until it is 3mm thick, cut disks with a round cutter 9cm in diameter. Place on greaseproof paper and chill in the fridge for 20 minutes.

Fry the sugar and butter until the mixture turns a dark caramel colour. Remove from the heat and divide the caramel into the muffin tins. Make sure the caramel coats the base of the tin. Add butternut mixture to each tin, pressing down firmly. Bake for ten minutes. Remove the puff pastry from the fridge. Remove the muffin tins from the oven and carefully place a puff pastry disc on top of each muffin, tucking in the edge of the pastry on the sides. Bake for another 15 minutes until the pastry is golden.

Cool the tatins in the tin, then invert onto a tray. Serve with shaved parmesan and a drizzle of Turkish balsamic (or ordinary balsamic vinegar if you can't find the Turkish variety).

butternut	**900g**
sprigs thyme	**2**
salt and black pepper	
puff pastry	**150g**
caster sugar	**75g**
butter	**30g**
shaved parmesan	**50g**
Turkish fig balsamic	
vinegar	**45ml**

It is important to keep puff pastry cold until it is placed over the filling so it crisps well

Calamari, Avocado and Fennel Skewers

12 KEBABS

black olives	**125ml**
small onion	**1**
olive oil	**125ml**
white wine vinegar	**60ml**
fennel leaves	**20ml**
Dijon mustard	**5ml**
lemon, zested	**1**
salt and black pepper	
calamari tubes	**600g**
calamari tentacles	**600g**
avocados	**2**
fennel bulbs	**2**
kebab skewers	**12**

Pit and chop the olives and mix them with the finely chopped onion in a small bowl. Pour in the olive oil, vinegar, chopped fennel leaves, mustard, lemon zest, salt and black pepper and stir together. Tip half the dressing into a jug and set aside.

Clean the calamari tubes, make a cut on one side of the tube and carefully score in a criss-cross pattern. Marinate the calamari tubes and tentacles in one third of the olive dressing for 30 minutes. Season. Heat a grill pan and fry the calamari for two minutes or until just cooked. Transfer to a plate and set aside to cool. Peel off the outer layer of the fennel and slice in half lengthways and then into four, depending on the size of your fennel. Peel and cube the avocados. Assemble the skewer with the calamari, fennel, calamari, avocado and calamari. Drizzle with dressing and serve.

If you can resist eating them straight out of the pan, these go well with a green salad

Courgette and Chickpea Fritters

SERVES **6**

FRITTERS:

courgettes	500g
onion	1
ground coriander	15ml
ground cumin	5ml
garlic cloves	2
chickpea flour	200ml
coriander leaves	60ml
sunflower oil	60ml

CUCUMBER RAITA:

full cream plain yoghurt	500ml
English cucumber	1
mint leaves	10ml
ground cumin	2ml
cayenne pepper	2ml
salt and black pepper	

Tip the yoghurt in a mixing bowl and whisk for two minutes. Seed and finely chop the cucumber and add it to the yoghurt with the chopped mint, cumin, cayenne pepper, salt and pepper. Mix well.

To make the fritters, grate the courgettes and mix them with the chopped onion, ground coriander, cumin, crushed garlic, chickpea flour, chopped coriander leaves, salt and pepper. Form into 12 balls. Heat a frying pan and fry the flattened courgette balls in batches for about two minutes on each side. Serve on a platter with the cucumber raita.

Raita is a yoghurt and cucumber sambal to go with curries and other oriental foods

Chorizo, Lentil and Peanut Pasties

MAKES 12

onions	**2**
carrots	**2**
chorizo	**200g**
garlic cloves	**2**
knob ginger	**1**
olive oil	**30ml**
red lentils	**125g**
chopped tomatoes	
	1 x 400g tin
raw peanuts	**100ml**
salt and black pepper	
mozzarella cheese	**100g**
basil leaves	**60ml**
quantity farmhouse	
pastry (page 136)	**half**
egg	**1**
milk	**30ml**
black sesame seeds	**30ml**

Finely chop the onions, carrots, chorizo, garlic and ginger. Heat the olive oil in a medium saucepan and fry the onions, carrots and chorizo until soft. Stir in the garlic and ginger, fry for one minute and add the lentils and tinned tomatoes. Add just enough water to cover. Bring to a gentle boil and simmer, covered, for 20 minutes. Stir occasionally, as lentils tend to stick easily. Remove from the heat, add the peanuts and set aside for 10 minutes. Season. Add the mozzarella and torn basil. Pre-heat the oven to 200°C.

Take the pastry out ten minutes before you need it and roll it out on a lightly floured work surface to about 3mm thick. Cut out 12 rings, 9cm in diameter.

Beat the egg and milk together and brush onto the pastry circles. Spoon a heaped teaspoon of filling onto the centre of each circle. Fold the pasties in half, gently pushing out any air and making sure the edges are sealed tightly by pressing with the back of a fork. Lightly brush with the remaining egg and milk mixture and sprinkle with sesame seeds. Place on a baking tray and bake for 25–30 minutes or until golden in colour.

Chicken Gyoza

FILLING:

chicken mince	400g
kejap manis	30ml
caster sugar	10ml
cornflour	10ml
egg	1
sesame oil	10ml
bunches spring onions	2
coriander leaves	60ml
red chillies	2

DIPPING SAUCE:

light soy sauce	125ml
rice wine vinegar	60ml
sweet chilli sauce	30ml
fish sauce	10ml

gyoza/wonton wrappers	40
sunflower oil	

Mix together the chicken mince, kejap manis, caster sugar, cornflour, beaten egg, sesame oil, finely chopped spring onion, torn coriander and chopped chillies in a large mixing bowl. Place in the fridge for an hour.

To make the dipping sauce, lightly whisk the soy sauce, vinegar, chilli sauce and fish sauce together. Check the seasoning and set aside.

To assemble, place a heaped teaspoon of chicken filling on each wrapper. Seal with a little water, pinching the sides together like you would a Cornish pasty but place them on their side. Heat a frying pan with water and poach the wrappers for two minutes. Remove them with a slotted spoon and drain on kitchen paper. Heat the oil and fry the wrappers until golden brown on medium heat. Serve with the dipping sauce.

Kejap manis is a lovely sweetened, thick soy sauce available from Chinese supermarkets or specialist food shops

Potted Trout

fennel seeds   **30ml**
butter   **500g**
zest and juice of lemon **1**
fresh fennel   **60ml**
capers   **100ml**
smoked trout fillets   **8**
salt and white pepper

Heat a small frying pan and lightly toast the fennel seeds. Grind them using a mortar and pestle. Tip the butter, zest and juice of the lemon and 45ml of the finely chopped fennel into a small saucepan and bring to a gentle boil. Remove from the heat and remove any scum that floats on top. Set aside for ten minutes. Discard the milk solids, which will have sunk to the bottom of the saucepan.

Pour three quarters of the butter mixture into a medium mixing bowl and place the remaining butter mixture in a jug. Flake the trout fillets and stir in with the remaining fennel, 80ml of the chopped capers, salt and pepper to taste. Stir gently, checking the seasoning. Spoon into eight ramekins, tapping down gently to remove air bubbles. Mix the remaining capers and butter together and gently spoon over the top. Refrigerate for an hour and serve with melba toast or thin slices of health bread.

Grilled Carrots with Aioli

SERVES 6

carrots	**250g**
olive oil	**45ml**

AIOLI:

garlic cloves	**16**
salt	
eggs	**2**
lemons	**2**
salt and white pepper	
extra virgin olive oil	
	600ml

To make the aioli, place the peeled garlic and a pinch of salt in a mortar and pestle and grind to a paste. Add the eggs, the juice of the lemons, salt and white pepper. Whisk well and slowly pour in the extra-virgin olive oil until you have a thick, dropping consistency. Check the seasoning and store in the fridge until needed. You will have more than you need for the grilled carrots but the aioli will last in the fridge for two weeks if not longer.

To prepare the carrots, bring a small saucepan of water to the boil and cook the carrots until tender. Drain and cut the carrots in half lengthways and place on a smoking grill pan drizzled with olive oil, salt and pepper. Grill until well coloured and serve on a platter with a bowl of aioli on the side. You can also cook these carrots on the braai.

Lamb Meatballs in Vine Leaves

MAKES 20

Rinse the vine leaves in cold water and reserve on a paper towel. Dry them well. Mix together the mince, Moroccan spice, cake flour, crushed garlic, chopped coriander, salt and pepper in a large bowl. Divide the mince mixture into 20 balls and roll tightly between your hands. Place each meatball onto a vine leaf with the veins facing you. Fold the sides of the leaves and roll them into sausage shapes to form parcels. Refrigerate for an hour to firm up.

Heat a grill pan on high heat. Brush a little olive oil over the parcels and grill for eight minutes on each side or until firm to the touch. Serve on a platter with a bowl of skordalia for dipping.

vine leaves	**20**
lamb mince	**1000g**
Moroccan spice	**60ml**
cake flour	**60ml**
garlic cloves	**4**
coriander leaves	**50ml**
salt and black pepper	
olive oil	
skordalia	**250ml**
(page 139)	

Taste a vine leaf first. If they're too salty, soak them in water for 15 minutes before use

FRIENDS FOR DINNER
CATERING WITH EASE

Sicillian Stuffed Pork Loin

SERVES 8

deboned pork loin 1800g
medium sweet potatoes 8

STUFFING:

olive oil	**45ml**
onions	**2**
garlic cloves	**2**
raisins	**200g**
pinenuts	**100g**
breadcrumbs	**80g**
Italian parsley	**20g**
salt and black pepper	

CREAMED SPINACH:

spinach bunches	**5**
eggs	**3**
cream	**400ml**
grated parmesan	**120g**
mascarpone	**100ml**
grated nutmeg	**2ml**

Pre-heat the oven to 200℃. Fry the chopped onion and crushed garlic in the olive oil until just starting to colour. Add the raisins, pine-nuts, breadcrumbs, parsley, salt and pepper and fry for a further two minutes. Cool for ten minutes. Lay the pork lion on your work surface. Where the pork loin meets the pork belly, cut with a sharp knife toward the top of the loin, leaving 2cm from the edge. Open the flap and spread the filling on the one side; fold the flap over to keep the stuffing sealed in. Roll tightly with string and season with salt, pepper and olive oil. Place a cake rack on the base of a roasting tray and rest the pork on top. Half fill the roasting tray with water. Turn the oven down to 180℃ and roast for an hour and a half.

Half an hour after you put the pork in the oven, drizzle the sweet potatoes with olive oil, season and add to the dish.

To make the creamed spinach, blanch the spinach in salted boiling water and refresh in iced water. Squeeze out the excess water. Roughly chop the spinach and mix with the eggs, cream, grated Parmesan, mascarpone, nutmeg, salt and pepper. Scrape into a small greased ovenproof dish and bake for 30 minutes or until cooked. Remove the pork from the oven and allow it to rest for 20 minutes. Remove the string and cut thick slices. Cut the sweet potato in half lengthways and place on a platter. Season with salt and pepper. Lay the sliced pork on top of the sweet potatoes, drizzle over a little of the pan juices and serve with the creamed spinach on the side.

Grilled Lamb Steaks with Sweet Potatoes

SERVES 6

Pre-heat the oven to 200°C. Roast the sweet potatoes, drizzled with a little olive oil and seasoned with salt and pepper, for 45 minutes or until they are tender.

Place the lamb in a mixing bowl and add the crushed garlic, lemon zest and juice, tomato puree, cumin, paprika, grape seed oil, grated onion and pepper and mix well. Cover with cling film to marinate for at least 30 minutes.

Season the steaks with salt. Heat a cast-iron pan and fry until medium rare (about five minutes, depending on the thickness).

Slice the sweet potatoes in half lengthways and place on a platter, season with salt and pepper, top with the rocket then the steaks. Pour the remaining juices over and serve.

lamb steaks	**500g**
rocket	**140g**
medium sweet potatoes	**6**
garlic cloves	**2**
lemon	**1**
tomato puree	**45ml**
ground cumin	**15ml**
paprika	**10ml**
grape seed oil	**30ml**
onion	**1**
salt and black pepper	

We like our lamb rare as it toughens quickly when cooked too much

Cumin-roasted Spatchcock Chicken

SERVES 6

whole chicken	**1600g**
olive oil	**45ml**
ground cumin	**10ml**
verjuice	**80ml**
salt and black pepper	
carrots	**450g**
new potatoes	**400g**
sprigs thyme	**2**
sprigs rosemary	**2**

RED ONION SALAD:

coriander leaves	**20g**
red onion	**1**
preserved lemon	
(page 136)	**1**

Pre-heat the oven to 200°C. To flatten the chicken for a spatchcock, cut down on the breastbone and push apart. Rub the chicken with 30ml olive oil, cumin, salt and pepper. Place in a shallow roasting tin and pour in 60ml verjuice. Scatter the sliced carrots lengthways on one side of the chicken and the new potatoes on the other. Scatter the herbs around and roast in the oven for 45 minutes.

Rest the chicken for ten minutes.

To make the salad, mix the chopped coriander, sliced onion and finely chopped skin of the preserved lemon with the remaining olive oil and verjuice. Season, stir well and set aside.

To serve, cut the chicken into pieces and place on a serving plate with the new potatoes. Mix the carrots with the salad and serve.

This is so quick and easy to prepare, leaving more time for socialising

Duck Leg Casserole

SERVES **6**

carrots	**14**
onion	**1**
leeks	**2**
duck leg and thigh joint	**6**
garlic cloves	**8**
vegetable stock	**1500ml**
dates	**100g**
sprigs thyme	**12**
sprigs parsley	**12**
bay leaves	**2**
whole chillies	
salt and black pepper	

Pre-heat the oven to 170°C. Peel and slice the carrots on the diagonal, 5mm thick. Slice the onion and the white of the leeks. Season the duck with salt and pepper and fry until browned on both sides. Remove and set aside. There should be enough fat remaining in the pan from cooking the duck – if not, add some olive oil. Fry the onion, leek and garlic for two minutes. Add the carrots and fry for five minutes before transferring to a casserole dish. Add the dates, thyme, parsley, bay and chilli before snuggling in the duck legs with the skin facing upwards. Barely cover with stock and place in the oven for an hour and a half or until the duck is tender and the sauce has thickened and reduced. Cover with foil if the duck is starting to burn. Remove from the oven and rest the casserole for ten minutes. Serve with crusty bread.

Szechwan Hot Fried Vegetables

cornflour	**10ml**
water	**15ml**
brinjals	**2**
carrot	**1**
green pepper	**1**
red pepper	**1**
garlic clove	**1**
knob ginger	**1**
broccoli florets	**200g**
sugar snap peas	**100g**
water chestnuts	**230g**
peanut oil	**45ml**
kejap manis	**30ml**
black bean sauce	**100ml**
Szechwan pepper mix	
(page 139)	**15ml**
cashew nuts	**75g**

Whisk the cornflour with the water and set aside. Cut the brinjals into long strips, slice the carrots, seed and slice the peppers into strips then drain and finely slice the water chestnuts. Heat the wok until smoking, then stir-fry the crushed garlic and chopped ginger in the peanut oil for a couple of seconds. Add the brinjals, carrots, green and red pepper and frying for two minutes. Add the sugar snap peas, broccoli and water chestnuts. Add the kejap manis, thicken the sauce with the cornflour liquid and cook for a couple of minutes. Add the black bean sauce, and Szechwan pepper and salt mix, and cook for another couple of minutes. Check the seasoning and sprinkle in the chopped cashew nuts.

Kejap manis is a sweetened, thick soy sauce which can be replaced with a normal soy sauce reduced at a simmer to half its volume.

Coconut Chicken on Spiced Cucumber

SERVES 8

coconut milk	**400ml**
balti curry paste	**60ml**
coriander leaves	**100ml**
chicken thighs	**16**
baby cucumber	**1kg**
olive oil	**60ml**
sesame oil	**90ml**
caster sugar	**10ml**
knobs ginger	**2**
garlic cloves	**4**
rice wine vinegar	**30ml**
red chillies	**3**
salt and black pepper	

Pre-heat the oven the to 200°C. Mix the coconut milk, balti paste and chopped coriander in a medium bowl and add the chicken. Allow to marinate for no less than 20 minutes.

Slice the cucumber diagonally into 5cm thick slices and set aside.

In a medium saucepan combine the oils, caster sugar, shredded ginger, crushed garlic, rice vinegar and two of the chillies, seeded and chopped, and bring to the boil. Remove from the heat and add the cucumbers. Season with salt and pepper.

Place the chicken on a roasting dish, pouring any leftover marinade into the dish. Season with a little sea salt and black pepper and roast for 30–35 minutes or until the chicken is cooked.

Spoon the cucumber onto a serving platter top with the chicken and garnish with a little extra coriander and finely chopped chilli.

Balsamic and Tomato Roasted Fish Fillets

SERVES 6

Pre-heat the oven to 200°C. Slice the brinjals into 1cm rounds. Heat a frying pan with 70ml of the oil and fry the rounds for two minutes on each side. Assemble six stacks of brinjals on a greased baking tray, top with the fish fillets and set aside.

Drain the tomatoes and squeeze out the seeds. Tip into a small bowl and stir in the vinegar, olive oil, sugar, salt and pepper. Spoon some of the tomatoes onto each fish fillet. Bake for 10–15 minutes or until cooked. Remove from the oven and serve with the torn basil leaves.

olive oil	100ml
brinjals	3
cape salmon fillets	6 x 200
whole tomatoes	1 x 400g tin
capers	60ml
balsamic vinegar	125ml
brown sugar	60ml
salt and black pepper	
basil leaves	100ml

This dish produces a lot of delicious pan dishes which beg to be served with crusty bread

Persian Lamb with Butternut SERVES 6

lamb knuckles	**1000g**
salt and	
ground black pepper	
olive oil	**80ml**
butternut	**800g**
cardamom pods	**8**
onions	**4**
ground cinnamon	**10ml**
ground cumin	**10ml**
honey	**10ml**
salt	**15ml**
chicken stock	**500ml**
saffron threads	**3ml**
pitted dates	**150g**
lemons, juiced	**2**
olive oil	**30ml**
mint leaves	**60ml**
roasted flaked	
almonds	**60ml**

Pre-heat the oven to 200°C. Place the lamb knuckles on a roasting tray and season with salt and pepper. Drizzle with olive oil. Roast for 20 minutes.

Meanwhile, peel the butternut and chop into 3cm cubes. Grind the cardamom pods in the mortar and pestle until you have a fine powder. Heat the oil in a large saucepan and fry the thinly sliced onions until soft and caramel in colour. Add the sealed lamb, cinnamon, cumin, cardamom, honey, salt and chicken stock. The lamb should be covered with the liquid, top up with chicken stock or water if need be. Bring the lamb to the boil and simmer for one hour. Steep the saffron in 30ml hot water for five minutes then add – with the dates and the juice of the lemons – to the casserole. Tip the butternut into a roasting tray and season with salt, pepper and drizzle over the olive oil. Roast for 30 minutes.

Simmer the lamb for a further 30 minutes or until it is tender. Carefully stir in the cooked butternut and garnish with the mint leaves and toasted almonds. Serve with warmed couscous.

Pumpkin, Sage and Feta Cannelloni

CREPES:

cake flour	400g
eggs	2
olive oil	30ml
milk	300ml
salt and black pepper	
sunflower oil	10ml

FILLING:

pumpkin	1500g
sage leaves	30ml
feta	150g
grated parmesan	150g
dried chilli flakes	2ml
garlic clove	1
grated nutmeg	2ml
butter	30g

TOPPING:

unsalted butter	150g
sage leaves	15

Pre-heat the oven to 180°C. For the crepes whisk together the flour, eggs, olive oil, salt and pepper to form a stiff paste, then whisk in the milk until you have a lump-free batter. Let the batter stand for ten minutes before cooking.

Heat a 20cm non-stick frying pan until hot. Turn down the heat to medium and add a little oil to coat the bottom of the pan. Pour 30ml of batter into the pan, swirling it around to coat the base. The crepe should be quite thin. Cook for two minutes on one side then slide it onto a square of greaseproof paper and continue to cook more crepes. You won't need any more oil as the batter already contains oil. Stack the crepes between sheets of greaseproof paper to separate. Set the crepes aside until needed.

Place the peeled and chopped pumpkin in a shallow roasting dish, drizzle with olive oil and season with salt and pepper. Roast for 30–45 minutes until tender. Scrape into a bowl, draining off all the liquid. Lightly mash the pumpkin with a fork, add the chopped sage and stir in the remaining ingredients until well combined and cool. Season to taste.

To assemble, place 12 crepes on the work surface and divide the pumpkin mixture between them. Roll each crepe into log shape, then place in a greased ovenproof and bake for 20 minutes.

To make the topping, place a frying pan on high heat. Add the butter and chopped sage leaves and cook over medium heat until the butter foams. Place two crepes onto each serving plate and spoon over the browned butter. Great served with salad leaves.

Resting the batter once mixed helps make more firm crepes

Grilled Kingklip on Chorizo Mash

kingklip fillets	**6**
salt	
ground black pepper	
olive oil	

DRESSING:

saffron	**2ml**
verjuice	**15ml**
plum tomatoes	**4**
red chilli	**1**
coriander seeds	**2ml**
ground cumin	**5ml**
small roasted	
red pepper	**1**
cloves garlic	**2**
olive oil	**150ml**
lemon	**half**
coriander leaves	**10ml**
mint leaves	**10ml**

TO SERVE:

quantity chorizo	
mashed	
potato (page 139)	**1**

Pre-heat the oven to 200°C. To make the dressing, steep the saffron in the verjuice for five minutes. Blanch, peel, slice and seed the tomatoes, then seed and finely chop the chilli. Roast the red pepper in the oven until the skin is slightly blackened. When they are cool enought to handle, peel them then seed and slice into strips. Place the saffron and verjuice, tomatoes, crushed coriander seeds, ground cumin, red pepper, chilli, chopped garlic, olive oil and lemon juice into a small saucepan and gently warm for ten minutes. Remove from the heat and set aside.

Place the kingklip fillets on a lightly greased baking tray. Season with salt and pepper and drizzle over a little olive oil. Place in the top half of the oven and cook for 15 minutes or until the fish is cooked through. Stir the chopped coriander, mint, salt and pepper into the tomato dressing. Check the seasoning and serve on mash with the dressing spooned over.

Chinese Barbeque Pork Ramen with Lime

SERVES 1

soy sauce	15ml
Chinese five-spice powder	2ml
beaten egg	15ml
Chinese barbeque sauce	10ml
caster sugar	15ml
honey	15ml
sake	15ml
pork loin	200g
chicken stock	350ml
miso paste	60ml
spinach leaves	4
egg noodles	125g
red chilli	half
spring onions	2
garlic clove	1
knob ginger	half
lime	1

Pre-heat the oven to 200°C. Mix the soy sauce, five-spice, egg, barbeque sauce, sugar, honey and sake in a small bowl. Remove any sinew from the pork and marinate for a minimum of 15 minutes. Roast in the oven for 15 minutes or until cooked, then rest for five minutes before slicing.

Heat the stock and dissolve the miso paste in it. Bring a saucepan of salted water to the boil and blanch the spinach leaves, then refresh in iced water. Cook the noodles for five minutes or until just tender. Slice the chilli and spring onion finely on the angle. Shred the ginger and crush the garlic, and set aside.

To serve place the noodles in the centre of a warm bowl. Pour in the miso stock, add some pork, spinach, chilli, spring onion and a squeeze of lime.

Chilli-roasted Beef Fillet on Bokh Choi

SERVES **6**

beef fillet	1600g
roasted chilli paste	45ml
peanut oil	30ml
kejap manis	45ml
chilli oil	15ml

SAUCE:

mushroom soy sauce	100ml
chicken stock	100ml
shaoshing wine	30ml
ginger	30ml
bunch spring onion	1
red chilli	2
caster sugar	5ml
sesame oil	5ml

GREENS:

bokh choi	6
peanut oil	15ml
garlic cloves	2
light soy sauce	15ml

Trim any sinew from the beef fillet and marinate with the chilli paste, peanut oil, kejap manis and chilli oil. Marinate for a minimum of 30 minutes. Pre-heat the oven to 200°C. Heat a frying pan and seal the fillet on all sides. Place on a roasting tray and roast for ten minutes. Rest for ten minutes before slicing.

For the sauce, place the mushroom soy, chicken stock, shaoshing wine, shredded ginger, spring onion, seeded and finely chopped chilli, caster sugar and sesame oil into a saucepan and bring to the boil. Simmer for ten minutes, check the seasoning and set aside.

For the greens, fill a wok with water and bring to the boil. Halve the bokh choi lengthways, place on a plate that will fit in a bamboo steamer. In a small bowl whisk the peanut oil, crushed garlic and soy together and pour over the greens. Steam for five minutes or until tender. Serve the sliced beef fillet on top of the greens with the sauce on the side.

Shaoshing is a rice wine for cooking which is standard in the Chinese kitchen

Flattened Cinnamon Quail

deboned quails	**12**

QUAIL MARINADE:

cinnamon	**15ml**
pomegranate syrup	**30ml**
ponzu sauce	**15ml**
soy sauce	**15ml**
zest of lemon	**1**
olive oil	**80ml**
carrots	**500g**
zest of lemon	**1**
knob ginger	**1**
olive oil	**50ml**
garlic clove	**1**
coriander leaves	**125ml**
salt and black pepper	
rocket	**250g**

For the marinade, mix the cinnamon, syrup, ponzu, soy, lemon zest and olive oil in a medium bowl. Add the quail and marinate, covered, for at least two hours.

Pre-heat the oven to 180°C. Stir together the peeled, sliced carrots, lemon zest, finely chopped ginger, olive oil and crushed garlic. Tip onto a roasting tray and roast for 30 minutes or until the carrots are tender. Remove from the oven and toss together with the coriander. Set the oven on grill. Lay the quail out on a baking sheet lined with tin foil and lightly greased with oil. Season the quail with salt and pepper and place under the grill for four minutes on each side. The marinade has a high sugar content and will caramelise, crisping the skin nicely. Serve the quail on top of the carrots with a side salad of rocket.

Ponzu is a citrus flavoured soy sauce, available in Chinese and specialist food stores

Indian Spiced Butternut and Peas in Red Pepper Sauce

SERVES 6

SAUCE:

red peppers	4
onion	1
knob ginger	1
garlic cloves	3
green chilli	1
water	225ml
ground almonds	25g
cumin seeds	15ml
coriander seeds	15ml
turmeric	5ml
cayenne pepper	2ml
lemon	1
salt	10ml
sunflower oil	90ml
black pepper	2ml
butternuts	2
frozen peas	500ml
coriander leaves	60ml
garam masala	30ml

For the sauce, seed the red peppers and process them with all the other sauce ingredients in a blender until smooth.

Heat the sunflower oil in a medium saucepan and tip in the pureéd pepper sauce. Fry for 10 minutes then add the black pepper and peeled, cubed butternut. Cover and simmer for 20 minutes or until the butternut is tender. Tip in the peas and serve garnished with coriander leaves and garam masala.

This dish like most Indian food is really about subtle flavours rather than heat

Prawns with Verjuice Dressing

SERVES **6**

Pre-heat the grill of the oven. Bring a large saucepan of salted water to the boil. Remove the flesh from the preserved lemon and finely chop the skin. Stir together the preserved lemon, chilli, crushed garlic, verjuice, 100ml of the olive oil, chopped parsley and torn basil. Check the seasoning and set aside.

Cook the pasta until al dente. Drain and toss with a little oil. Season with salt and pepper.

Butterfly the prawns and remove the vein. Place the butterflied prawns onto a baking tray and season with salt, pepper and drizzle 80ml of olive oil. Place under the grill for five minutes until cooked. Place the linguine on the base of a platter, top with the prawns and drizzle over the preserved lemon dressing.

linguine	**500g**
tiger prawns	**700g**
olive oil	**180ml**

DRESSING:

preserved lemons (page 136)	**3**
crushed chilli	**2ml**
garlic cloves	**2**
verjuice	**100ml**
olive oil	**180ml**
Italian parsley	**60ml**
basil leaves	**60ml**
salt and black pepper	

Basics
SOME SIMPLE THINGS YOU'LL NEED TO KNOW

Sweet Pastry

cake flour	**250g**
cold butter	**100g**
icing sugar	**100g**
eggs	**2**

Tip the flour, chopped butter and icing sugar into a large mixing bowl. Rub the butter between your fingers until the mixture resembles fine breadcrumbs. Lightly whisk the eggs and add to the flour mixture. Stir until the dough comes together. Tip the dough onto a lightly floured surface and bring the dough together to form a flattish ball. Wrap in cling film and place in the fridge for an hour. This is quite a sticky pastry and it firms up in the fridge. You vary it by adding orange or lemon zest, crushed cardamom or 50g of cocoa and 50g icing sugar instead of the 100g icing sugar.

Farmhouse Pastry

cake flour	**700g**
brown sugar	**40g**
sea salt	**5ml**
baking powder	**5ml**
cold butter	**500g**
eggs	**2**
white wine vinegar	**30ml**
ice cold water	**125ml**

Tip the cake flour, brown sugar, salt, baking powder and chopped butter into a large mixing bowl. Rub with your fingers until the mixture resembles fine breadcrumbs. Whisk the eggs, vinegar and water together and pour into the butter mixture. Stir the ingredients together until it starts to come together to form a ball. Tip the dough onto a lightly floured surface and lightly knead for one minute. Divide into two and wrap in cling film. Place in the fridge for 30 minutes before rolling out. The pastry will last for five days in the fridge or you can freeze it until needed.

Preserved Lemons

lemons	**3**
sea salt	**135ml**
olive oil	**15ml**
black peppercorns	**6**
sprigs thyme	**2**
boiling water	

Sterilize a jar that will hold the lemons tightly by placing the bottle in a pre-heated oven at 160°C for 20 minutes. Cut the lemons into quarters, leaving an inch from the bottom of the lemon. Fill the cavities of the lemons with the sea salt and place them into the sterilised jar. Pour the olive oil, peppercorns and thyme into the jar and cover the lemons with boiling water. Seal the jar and store in the fridge for at least four weeks before use. We store our bottled preserved lemons in the fridge due to the high humidity in KwaZulu-Natal.

Classic Pesto

flaked almonds	100g
basil leaves	50g
Italian parsley	100g
garlic cloves	4
olive oil	250ml
salt and black pepper	
parmesan	100g

Toast the almonds until golden in a frying pan or under the grill. Place the almonds, basil leaves, chopped parsley, and peeled garlic into the blender and blitz until roughly chopped. Add the olive oil in two batches, scraping down the sides of the bowl on each occasion. Scrape into a bowl and stir in the grated parmesan. Check the seasoning and store in a sterilized jar. Cover the pesto with a film of olive oil. This will act as a natural preservative. Store in the fridge until needed. The pesto will last about two months. Try and change the herbs, add chopped chillies, change the nuts.

Couscous

SERVES 4

couscous	500g
vegetable stock	600ml
salt and black pepper	
butter	30g
bunch spring onions	1
Italian parsley	30g

SERVES 4

Place the couscous, salt, pepper and butter in a medium bowl. Pour over the boiling vegetable stock and stir with a fork to mix the ingredients together. Set aside for ten minutes. Finely slice the spring onions and finely chop the parsley. Fluff the couscous with a fork or between your fingers to help loosen the grains. Stir the herbs into the couscous, check the seasoning and serve. This is your basic recipe for couscous; you can add roasted peppers, olives and feta or a combination of pumpkin seeds, sunflower seeds and sesame seeds.

Vanilla Egg Custard

egg yolks	6
caster sugar	90g
milk	500ml
cream	100ml
vanilla pod	1

Split the vanilla pod in half with a sharp knife and place in a medium saucepan with the milk. Gently bring the milk to a gentle boil. Place the egg yolks and the sugar into a medium bowl and whisk until the texture is thick and pale in colour. Pour the hot milk onto the egg yolks and sugar and whisk together. Place back on the heat and stir with a wooden spoon on medium heat until the custard coats the back of the spoon. Strain the custard through a sieve into a clean bowl and stir for two minutes; dust the surface with icing sugar as this prevents a skin forming. Cool and place in the fridge until needed.

Basics
SOME SIMPLE THINGS YOU'LL NEED TO KNOW

Chicken Stock   3,5l

leeks	2
carrots	2
celery stalks	2
onion	1
head garlic	1
black peppercorns	5
sprigs thyme	6
parsley stalks	8
bay leaves	2
whole chicken	1
litres water	4

Cut the leeks in half lengthways and wash off any dirt that may be in. Roughly chop the carrots, celery, onion and slice the garlic in half. Tip the cut vegetables into a large saucepan with the peppercorns, thyme, parsley, bay leaves, chicken and water. The chicken must be completely covered with water. Bring the stock to the boil and simmer gently for 60 minutes or until the chicken is cooked. Skim off any scum that rises to the surface. Once the stock is ready remove the chicken from the saucepan and drain the stock. Use what you need for your recipe and freeze the rest. It will keep for up to four days in the fridge. Use the chicken for sandwiches or a chicken pie.

Vegetable Stock   3l

olive oil	45ml
onion	1
head of garlic	1
leeks	2
celery sticks	2
butternut	1/2
tomatoes	2
bay leaf	1
parsley stalks	8
sprigs thyme	4
litres water	4
salt	5ml

Heat the olive oil in a large saucepan and fry the peeled and chopped onion, garlic, sliced leek, celery and roughly chopped butternut and fry for five minutes. Add the chopped tomatoes, bay leaf, parsley, thyme, water and salt. Bring to the boil and simmer for 45 minutes, skim off any impurities that rise to the surface. Strain the stock through a fine sieve. Cool and place in the fridge or freeze until needed.

Mayonnaise   500ml

egg yolks	4
Dijon mustard	15ml
salt and white pepper	
white wine vinegar	60ml
sunflower oil	250ml
olive oil	250ml
hot water	15ml

Place the egg yolks, Dijon mustard, salt, white pepper and vinegar in a food processor. Blitz for ten seconds. With the motor running pour in the sunflower oil, then the olive oil in a thin stream until the mayonnaise becomes thick. Lastly pour in the hot water as this helps to stabilize the mayonnaise. Check the seasoning and keep in the fridge until needed in a sealed container.
You may flavour your mayonnaise with saffron steeped in a little olive oil and substitute the white wine vinegar with lemon juice. Try different mustards or add chopped herbs.

Mashed Potato

SERVES 6

large potatoes   **1500g**
olive oil   **45ml**
salt and white pepper

Peel and roughly chop the potatoes and place them in a sauce-pan covered with water and seasoned with salt. Bring to the boil and simmer until tender. Drain the potatoes and mash through a potato ricer. Beat the olive oil into the potatoes with a wooden spoon for 2 minutes, as this will give you a light and fluffy mash potato. Season with salt and pepper.

Flavour the mash with a couple tablespoons of pesto or a wholegrain mustard. For chorizo mash, remove the skin from one chorizo sausage and roughly chop. Peel and crush two garlic cloves and fry with the chorizo in olive oil until it start to brown then stir into the mash.

Cheesy Wet Polenta

SERVES 4

chicken stock   **1500ml**
salt and black pepper
butter   **30ml**
quick cook polenta   **225g**
parmesan   **115g**

Pour the chicken stock, butter and salt into a medium sauce-pan. Bring to the boil and slowly pour in the polenta in a steady stream, whisking all the time. Change to a wooden spoon and stir the polenta until it's cooked — this will take about five minutes. Remove the polenta from the heat and stir in the grated parmesan, season with black pepper and check the seasoning and serve.

Polenta is wheat-free option for starch and you can vary the flavour by adding chopped herbs, pesto, feta, olives or even pan-fried chicken livers.

Skordalia

potatoes   **450g**
garlic cloves   **3**
white wine vinegar   **7ml**
extra virgin olive oil   **175ml**
cream   **30ml**

Peel and roughly chop the potatoes, tip into a medium saucepan and cover with water. Season with salt and bring to the boil. Simmer until the potatoes are tender. Drain the potatoes and mash them through a ricer. Add the peeled and crushed garlic, salt, pepper and vinegar. Beating with a wooden spoon, slowly add the olive oil and then the cream. Check the seasoning and serve warm with the vine wrapped lamb meatballs, braaied meats or as a snack with toasted tortilla chips.

Café Latte 13-	Milkshake 15-	~~Muffins 10~~
Espresso 9-50	Horlicks Shake 17-	Sandwiches - Meat or veg 2
Double Espresso 14-	Ice Teas 11-	Pukka Chai available
Mocciato 10-50	Coke - Tab - Sprite 8-50	
Hot Chocolate 14-	Valpré 8-	
Horlicks 14-	Fruit Juice 11-	Buffet Lunch
Ceylon Tea 10-	Fruit & Yog Shake 11-	R85 per kg
Earl Grey 10-	Frappe 14-	
Milo 14-	Fruit Teas 11-	
Choccoccino 14-	Rooibos 10-	
Decaf or skinny available		Please place order at the counte

list of recipes

RUSSEL WASSERFALL

With a background in advertising as both copywriter and creative director, Russel Wasserfall picked up a camera in 1999 and decided he wanted to be a food photographer. He was running a sushi bar with a couple of friends at the time and it seemed a logical next step. Also, he was already being driven mad by all the phone calls from super-models, so he didn't want to be a fashion photographer. His skills as a writer are never far from any project he tackles, and on this - his third cook book in as many years - he wrote, photographed and project-managed the book for his dear friends and fellow foodies, Clare and Fiona Ras.

LUANNE TOMS

From Art Directing magazines, such as Elle Decoration, to designing a cook book for Sprigs, Luanne has a great passion for publishing. She love being involved in all areas of the creative process, from the initial concept design, through to styling and Art Directing. This is especially true of the Sprigs cook book. Luanne currently freelances as a designer, art directing and styling for various magazines and clients.

In this book, we set out to find the essence of Sprigs. Clare and Fiona made this an incredible project to work on because their food is simple and honest and they are straight-forward, hard working and easy to get along with. The result therefore is a very real, no fuss, honest cook book with loads of soul.

SPRIGS

FRESH KITCHEN INSPIRATION

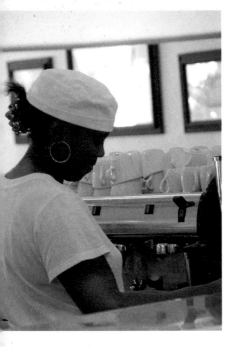

Olive
Tapenade

olive

• Scrambled egg, bacon on toast 21-50
• Omelette of the day   26-
• Fruit Breakfast   26-
• French toast with   28-50
• Special Breakfast   36-

SPRIGS
THE FOOD SHOP

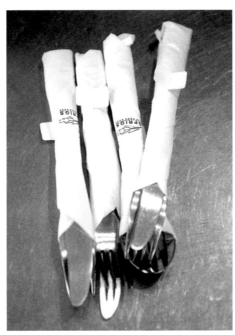

SPRIGS
THE FOOD SHOP

SPRIGS